About me

School: ....

Class: ....

Teacher: ....

First language(s): ....

Other language(s): ....

Write your favourite words in different languages.

English ....

My language skills

1 Draw the pictures in the spaces below.

Listening		🙂
Reading		🙂
Speaking		🙂
Writing		🙂

2 Do you like doing these things in English?
  Colour the faces. Blue = It's good. Green = It's OK.

I can ...   Units 1-3

1 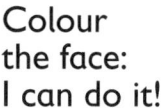 Listen and colour.

2 How do you spell ...?

3 Read and match.

camera bike lorry robot computer game kite

4 Write.

My favourite toys are _____

_____ .

Colour the face: I can do it!
1 
2 
3 
4 

I can ...   # Units 4-6

<table>
<tr><td>Colour the face:
I can do it!</td></tr>
</table>

1 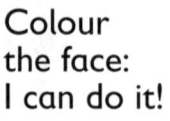 **Listen and point.**

1
☺

2  **Tell your partner about your family.**

> My family is small. I've got ...

2
☺

3  **Read and match.**

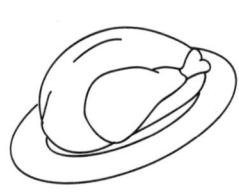  

bread   water   juice   chips   chicken   rice   egg   milk

   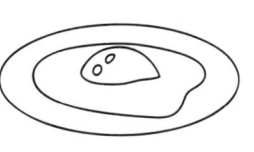

3
☺

4  Write about your favourite lunch.

4
☺

I can ...

Units 7-9

1  Listen and point.

1

2 💬 Point and say.
Use 'in', 'on', 'next to', 'under' and 'between'.

2

3 🔍 Look at the picture. Tick (✓) or cross (✗) the boxes.

3

1   The park is between the toy shop and the café. ☒
2   There's a doll and a car in the toy shop. ☐
3   There's a street and there's a park. ☐
4   The monkey is under the tree. ☐
5   There's a hospital next to the café. ☐
6   The ball is on the table. ☐

4 ✏️ Write about your favourite clothes.

4

I can... Units 10-12

1 Listen. Say 'yes' or 'no'.

1

2 Point and say.

2

3 Read and circle the pictures above.
What would Ben like?

I'd like some lemonade and a sausage. Oh, and I'd like some watermelon, please!

3

4 Write.

I can see _____

and _____ in the mountains.

I can see _____

and _____ at the beach.

4

6

English and me

I learn English …

… at school ☑
… at home (private classes) ☐
… at an academy ☐
… in the summer holidays ☐

My favourite English activities are:

listening ☐ reading ☐ speaking ☐ writing ☐
games ☐ songs ☐ using the book ☐

I speak English to my _____ .

An English song I like: _____

An English book I like: _____

An English film I like: _____

People speak English in _____ .
I want to go there on holiday!

My school bag

Draw your school bag. What's inside it?
Colour your picture.

My school bag

Now write about your school bag.

My bedroom

Draw a picture or stick a photo of your bedroom.

My bedroom

Have you got these things in your bedroom?
Write 'yes' or 'no'.

phone _____   mirror _____   armchair _____   guitar _____

bookcase _____   computer _____   cupboard _____   toys _____

lamp _____   mat _____   clock _____   window _____

What have you got in your bedroom?

_____

My family

Draw a picture of you and your family.

My family

The people in my picture/photo are:

How old are they?

My _____ is _____ years old.

My _____ is _____ years old.

Things I love

Draw or stick pictures of things you love.

I love ...

My favourite food is _____ .

My favourite sport is _____ .

My favourite animal is _____ .

My favourite _____ is _____ .

I love _____ !

My favourite clothes

Draw or stick pictures of your favourite clothes.

My favourite T-shirt.　　My favourite shoes.

My favourite _____

12

A holiday

Draw or stick a picture from your holiday.

My holiday

What people, things and places are in your picture?

Write about your holiday.

Second Edition

Kid's Box 2
Language Portfolio

This Language Portfolio allows your pupils to build a record of their progress through the school year.

The content follows the units of **Kid's Box** and the structure corresponds to that outlined by the Council of Europe's European Language Portfolio.

Please visit our website to download the Language Portfolio teaching notes.

www.cambridge.org/kidsbox

CAMBRIDGE
UNIVERSITY PRESS

ISBN 978-1-107-67499-8

9 781107 674998 >